THE GIFT
OF RECONCILIATION

THE GIFT
OF RECONCILIATION

For Parents of Children
Celebrating First Penance

MARY KATHLEEN GLAVICH, SND

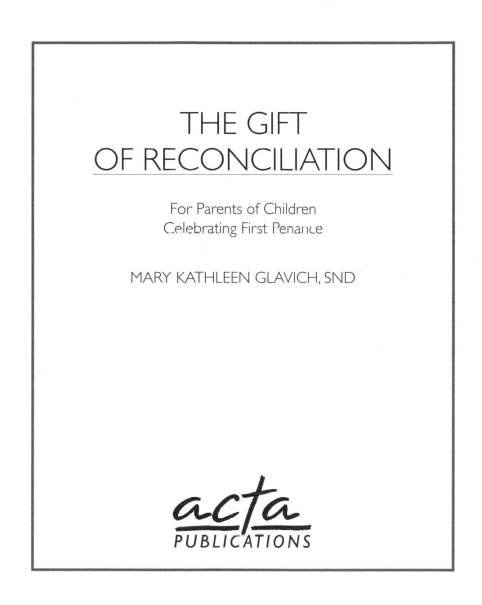

acta
PUBLICATIONS

THE GIFT OF RECONCILIATION
For Parents of Children Celebrating First Penance
by Mary Kathleen Glavich, SND

Edited by Joel Schorn
Cover design by Tom A. Wright
Typesetting by Patricia A. Lynch

Scripture excerpts are taken from the *New American Bible with Revised New Testament and Psalms*, copyright © 1991, 1986, 1970 by the Confraternity of Christian Doctrine, Inc., Washington D.C. Used with permission. All rights reserved. No part of the New American Bible may be reproduced by any means without permission in writing from the copyright owner.

Published by: ACTA Publications, 4848 N. Clark Street, Chicago, IL 60640, 800-397-2282, www.actapublications.com

Library of Congress Catalog Number: 2002092797
ISBN: 978-087946-234-5
Printed in the United States of America by Versa Press
Year: 18 17 16 15 14 13 12 11 10
Printing: 15 14 13 12 11 10 9 8 7 6

CONTENTS

Let us set things right, says the LORD:
Though your sins be like scarlet,
they may become white as snow;
Though they be crimson red,
they may become white as wool.

Isaiah 1:18

MAKING THINGS RIGHT

DEAR PARENTS,

Our world cries out for peace and reconciliation. The news is filled with stories of countries and peoples at war. Conflict also exists between races, neighbors, coworkers and relatives. If your family is normal, its members occasionally hurt one another and live in pain and tension for days, even years. As a result of sin, relationships are broken on all levels: relationships with God, with other people, and with self.

Your child will soon celebrate for the first time the gift God has given us to help bring about healing and peace: the sacrament of penance, or reconciliation.

In great love and mercy, God, through Jesus, has provided this way to ease the suffering that comes from sin and help prevent it in the future. God always enables us to make a fresh start. Because you have seen to it that your child was baptized, he or she can participate in this sacrament. Your child, for the rest of his or her life, can share in the gift through which God repairs relationships and brings peace to the heart.

It is your unique privilege and responsibility to prepare your child to encounter Jesus in the sacrament of penance. You have entrusted religion teachers to help you with this task. Your role, however, has a far more powerful impact than anyone else's. Your attitudes toward this sacrament and the way you model forgiveness and ask forgiveness from your child leave a lasting impression. Through your guidance your child can come to understand and appreciate the sacrament of reconciliation not as a burden but as a gift. He or she will approach the sacrament not in fear or solely out of obligation, but in joy and gratitude.

The explanations and activities in this book are intended to help you lead your child to God, who is our compassionate Father. Jesus assures us that God welcomes sinners with open arms, pardons us, and rejoices over our return.

If you are not up-to-date on church teaching regarding the sacrament of reconciliation, or if you are not Catholic, this book will be a valuable source of information—and perhaps inspiration—for you.

May the Holy Spirit be with you as you walk with your child on this stage of life's journey. When your child makes wrong moral decisions, may he or she always receive the grace to turn to God with confidence and trust. That way your child will live in peace and joy as a holy child of God. Then he or she will contribute to the world's peace and justice—the hallmarks of God's kingdom.

OUR NEED FOR FORGIVENESS

We live in an imperfect world with imperfect people. Why does the same world that has glorious sunsets also have earthquakes and tornadoes? Why are talented and creative people also marked by pride or greed? Why do marriages and friendships fall apart? Why can all of us say with Saint Paul, "I do not do the good I want, but I do the evil I do not want" (Romans 7:19)? Sin is a shared human experience. Some disaster at the beginning of time must have spoiled God's good creation. The Bible presents this concept through the story of the fall of Adam and Eve.

Our first parents were intended to share life and love forever with God their creator. Unfortunately Adam and Eve opposed God and rejected God's friendship and plan for them. This was the first sin. Because the original couple represented the human race, their sin shattered our relationship with our creator too.

The good God, however, offers us a second chance. As a loving Parent, God sent Jesus to repair the damage sin has done. Through the death and resurrection of Jesus, all sin was atoned for and forgiven: the original sin of Adam and Eve, our collective sin, and our personal sin. Moreover, in his mission as a Jewish preacher Jesus taught us by his words and by his own actions how to live in right relationships.

Following Jesus is not easy because the scars of the original offense remain. We are weakened and do not always choose what is good. We are not always loving. In other words, we sin against God, others and ourselves. The Hebrew word for sin is literally translated as "missing the mark." When we sin, our aim is off. We do not act as the reasonable, loving human beings we were meant to be. We sin in small ways (venial sin) and in serious ways (mortal, or deadly, sin). By mortal sin we sever ourselves completely from God.

Every time we pray the Creed we declare that we believe in the forgiveness of sins. God always gives us the opportunity to start over with a clean slate. We can do this through the prayers and ministry of the church. Whether or not we do so is up to us.

ILL EFFECTS OF SIN

Recall a time when you sinned. How did you feel afterwards? If you have a healthy, informed conscience, you probably felt guilt, remorse and shame—all uncomfortable feelings. These negative feelings can affect our mental and physical health. In addition, sin is divisive. It isolates us from God and other people.

By giving us the sacrament of penance Jesus offered us a way out of this painful situation, a way to live fully again. Russian Orthodox Christians refer to this sacrament as the "kiss of Christ."

Your child knows when he or she has done wrong and experiences the effects as keenly as you. Celebrating the sacrament of reconciliation will bring relief and joy to his or her heart too. For good reason another name for this sacrament is the sacrament of peace.

THE BALM OF FORGIVENESS

We have an innate desire to be forgiven, to be united with God and others again. Yet asking forgiveness is one of the most difficult tasks we must learn as human beings. Recently countries have been asking forgiveness for sins against groups of people. The church herself has felt the need to apologize for mistakes made in the past. Occasionally a great act of forgiveness catches the world's attention: The pope forgives the man who tried to assassinate him, a cardinal forgives the man who falsely accused him of sexual misdeeds, a spouse forgives a spouse for infidelity, a parent of a murdered child forgives the murderer. Reconciliation—forgiving and being forgiven—plays an important role in history and human life.

If anyone does sin,
we have an Advocate with the Father,
Jesus Christ the righteous one.
He is expiation for our sins,
and not for our sins only
but for those of the whole world.

I John 2:1-2

JESUS CHRIST, THE RECONCILER

If there is one word that characterizes Jesus, it is *merciful*. He came on a mission of mercy to help our fallen race. Through the paschal mystery—his suffering, death, resurrection and ascension—Jesus redeemed us. His atonement (at-one-ment) made us one with God again.

When questioned why he ate with sinners and tax collectors, Jesus declared, "Those who are well do not need a physician, but the sick do. I did not come to call the righteous but sinners" (Mark 2:17). Jesus befriends sinners and offers them salvation.

Jesus preached that God is merciful. Looking at Jesus, we see God in action. Over and over Jesus offered mercy to sinners. He demonstrated that his lessons and stories about a merciful God were true.

PROCLAIMING GOD'S MERCY
Three parables or stories Jesus told illustrate God's eagerness to welcome a sinner home. He said that God is like a shepherd who leaves ninety-nine sheep behind to search for one who has wandered off. When he finds the lost sheep, he carries it home with great joy and then calls his friends and neighbors together to rejoice with him. Jesus assured us that those in heaven rejoice whenever a sinner repents.

To make sure that we get the point, Jesus delivered the same message in another story. This time he compared God to a woman who owns ten silver coins and loses one. The woman lights a lamp, sweeps her house and searches until she finds the lost coin. Then she calls her friends and neighbors over to celebrate with her.

In case we still miss the message, Jesus packaged it in one of the most beloved stories in scripture, the story of the prodigal son. One day a son asks his father for his share of the inheritance (quite a crass thing to do!). The father agrees and bestows his inheritance prematurely. The boy leaves with his share and squanders every bit of it in a distant country. When a famine comes, the boy is forced to take a job tending swine (animals that Jewish people considered unclean). He is so hungry that he would even eat the pigs' fodder if someone offered it to him. Finally the wayward son comes to his senses and realizes that his father's workers are better off than he is. He decides to return home, admit his sin, and work for his father. The story goes that the father saw his son coming when he was still a long way off and was filled with compassion. (He must have been watching and yearning for the boy.) The man runs to his son (an undignified thing for a landowner to do), embraces him, and kisses him. Before the boy can finish his speech, the father orders the servants to bring the finest robe, a ring and sandals for him. He tells them to slaughter a calf for a feast in celebration. The father declares, "This son of mine was dead, and has come to life again; he was lost, and has been found" (Luke 15:24). It's been suggested that this parable be renamed the story of the prodigal father since the father is really the prodigal, or lavish, one in the story.

A modern version of this story is about a boy who regrets leaving his dad and writes a letter asking to come home. The son says that he will pass by the house and if he sees a yellow ribbon on a tree, he will know that the father will accept him back. The son hitchhikes home, and in the end is picked up by a truck driver. As the boy nears his house, he is afraid to look at the orchard.

He asks the trucker to tell him if there is a yellow ribbon tied to a tree. The man responds, "Son, there is a yellow ribbon on every tree in the orchard!" Such is God's eagerness to welcome a sinner home.

Knowing our heavenly Father's desire to forgive, Jesus taught us to pray in the Lord's Prayer, "Forgive us our trespasses."

MERCY IN ACTION

Jesus extended mercy to many people who had sinned against others and against him:

- Jesus forgave a woman who was caught in adultery and prevented her accusers from stoning her to death, the punishment Jewish law called for (John 8:1-11).
- Jesus said to a paralytic, "Your sins are forgiven," and then proceeded to heal him physically as well (Matthew 9:27).
- Jesus reached out to Zacchaeus, a Jewish man who collected taxes for Rome, the oppressor, and lined his own pockets with the profits. Jesus invited himself to dinner at Zacchaeus' house. The notorious sinner promised to give to the poor half of what he owned and to pay back four times the amount he stole (Luke 19:1-10).
- At a well in Samaria Jesus transformed a woman with a scandalous reputation into a successful disciple (John 4:4-42).
- Jesus forgave a sinful woman, who in sorrow for her sins washed his feet with her tears in public. He explained to critics that she love much because she was forgiven much (Luke 7:36-50).
- At the end of his life, Jesus forgave the thief on the cross next to him and promised him paradise (Luke 23:39 43).
- Hanging on the cross, Jesus prayed for his persecutors, "Father, forgive them, they know not what they do" (Luke 23:34).
- Although all but one of his closest followers deserted him in his hour of need, Jesus forgave them and entrusted his church into their hands. After the resurrection he appeared to the apostles and his first words were, "Peace be with you" (John 20:19).

- Even after Peter denied knowing him three times in order to save his own skin, Jesus forgave Peter and made him the head of the church. Jesus even gave Peter the opportunity to make up for his sin. Three times Jesus asked him, "Do you love me?" and three times Peter declared, "You know that I love you" (see John 21:15-17).

Jesus knew what it was to be tempted, but he never sinned. He does, however, show an extraordinary compassion toward those who do sin—including us.

HISTORY OF THE SACRAMENT

The roots of our sacrament of reconciliation go back to the Garden of Eden where human beings first learned to know what is good and what is bad. Since then we have always needed God's forgiveness.

The Old Testament is woven through and through with God's mercy to the Israelites. After God saved them from slavery in Egypt and made them his chosen people, they created a golden calf and worshipped it as their god. After God gave the Israelites the Promised Land, they turned to other gods repeatedly and then repented and asked forgiveness. Never tiring of taking them back, God forgave them over and over.

To express sorrow for sin, the Israelites offered prayer and animal or agricultural sacrifices and paid fines. Each year they observed a solemn day of repentance called Yom Kippur (Day of Atonement). On this day alone the high priest entered the Holy of Holies in the Temple to offer incense and seek atonement for the people. A communal ritual on Yom Kippur was to take a goat, symbolically load it with everyone's sins, and banish it to the demon who lived in the desert. This is the origin of our word *scapegoat*.

SCRIPTURAL BASIS

The basis for our formal ritual, which requires the mediation of a priest, is the directive of Jesus to the apostles. According to scripture, Jesus said to Peter, "I will give you the keys to the kingdom of heaven. Whatever you bind on earth shall be bound in heaven; and whatever you loose on earth shall be loosed in heaven" (Matthew 16:19). After Jesus rose from the dead, he appeared to his handpicked band, gathered in fear in the upper room. He greeted them with "Peace be with you." Then he breathed on them and said, "Receive the holy Spirit. Whose sins you forgive are forgiven them, and whose sins you retain are retained" (John 20:22-23).

Only God has the power to forgive sins, but the church established a method for our reconciliation to occur that makes the process more personal, warm and concrete. Through Jesus' representative we hear the words of forgiveness and are exhorted to do better. We believe that the power to act in the place of Jesus in forgiving sins has been transferred from the apostles to the bishops and priests who have succeeded them.

One advantage of the sacrament of reconciliation is hearing the words of absolution. They assure us that we are forgiven. There is nothing vague or questionable about it.

The sacrament also satisfies our need to ask forgiveness of another human being. Sin has repercussions on all of us. We are all a little worse for any one person's sin. In addition, sin alienates us from others. Therefore, expressing sorrow to a representative of the human race is just and right.

THE CHANGING FORMAT

In the early church only adults were admitted to baptism. It was regarded as the sacrament of conversion that totally turned one to God. It indicated a complete change of life. In this primary sacrament all sins committed prior to baptism were forgiven (just as they still are today). It was assumed that the newly baptized would maintain their baptismal innocence, but people began postponing their baptism as near to their death as possible to be sure that all their sins were forgiven.

In time, Christians who committed a serious sin (such as adultery, murder or heresy) after baptism could seek forgiveness by joining a special group called penitents. These people did public penance, sometimes for years. They wore sackcloth and ashes and could not receive Communion. The church prayed for them. On Holy Thursday, penitents were absolved and reconciled with the church. This public penance could happen only once in a lifetime, however.

It was the Irish monks of the eighth century who gave the sacrament the private form we know today. They organized the sacrament so that penitents confessed individually and privately to a priest. Moreover, this form of penance could be repeated.

In 1451, the Council of Trent confirmed that penance was a sacrament. It required that mortal sins be confessed to a priest who could give absolution in the name of Christ. The Second Vatican Council (1962-1965) made the sacrament more user-friendly by introducing the option of face-to-face confession. It also approved three rites for the sacrament, which are explained on pages 35-38.

Though the mountains leave
their place and the hills be shaken,
My love shall never leave you
nor my covenant of peace be shaken,
says the LORD, who has mercy on you.

Isaiah 54:10

THE HEALING PROCESS

Six-year-old Jessica looks at her younger brother Tom's artwork and exclaims, "That's a dumb picture. Who ever heard of purple grass? And your people look like monsters!" Tom's eyes well up with tears, his lips quiver, he socks Jessica in the arm and runs screaming from the room. Mom comes in from the kitchen and begins the repair work.

"Jessica, can't you two play nicely? He's just learning to draw. You used to make pictures like that too. That was a mean thing to say to Tommy, wasn't it?"

Jessica nods her head and says, "I guess so."

"How do you think Tommy feels?" Mom asks.

"Bad," Jessica replies.

"And how do you feel?" Mom continues.

"Bad," says Jessica. "I'm sorry I hurt his feelings."

"What do you think you should do?"

"Tell him I'm sorry."

"And what else?" Mom prods.

"Tell him I'll never do it again."

"How can you make it up to him?"

"I can give him my new box of crayons."

"Yes," Mom encourages, "and maybe you can offer to help him draw. Let's go see him now."

Together they go to smooth over the latest family crisis.

Scenarios like this occur daily in family life. Just as most accidents happen in the home, most sins happen in the home. We are constantly called to reconcile with family members. Reconciliation is the glue that holds all relationships together.

The previous story contains the main elements of the process of reconciliation:

- acknowledging one's sin,
- confessing it,
- contrition,
- intending to avoid the sin in the future,
- making up.

ACKNOWLEDGING ONE'S SIN

Jesus told a parable about two men who went to the Temple to pray. One man prayed, "I thank you, Lord, that I am not like the rest of humanity or like that tax collector over there. I fast and pay tithes." In contrast, the tax collector, with eyes lowered, simply prayed, "O God, be merciful to me, a sinner" (Luke 18:9-14). Jesus asked who went home justified. Often we are like the first man. We are blind to our own sins and faults. Jesus knew this. He once asked, "Why do you notice the splinter in your brother's eye but do not perceive the wooden beam in your own eye?" (Matthew 7:3).

Our pride and self-esteem make us resist seeing ourselves as sinners. We like to envision ourselves as ideal. It pains us to have to admit that we sometimes fail. Yet only by admitting our sins can we hope to overcome them and be free from them.

You can assist your child in taking this step first by teaching what is right and what is wrong. Gradually you will be forming your child's conscience. Conscience is not a voice within nor a supernatural power. Rather it is the power of our mind to judge the morality of an act. Point out when your child is not loving but offending God and hurting others. Discourage holding grudges and getting even. On the other hand, praise and reward your child after a virtuous act. When viewing movies or reading books with your child discuss the morality of the characters' actions. With your prompting and guidance, your child will develop a conscience that detects sin and bothers him or her after a sin has been committed.

CONFESSING SIN

Stating one's sin aloud to another person is therapeutic. It is a powerful step on the way to healing. Kept inside, sin festers and causes multiple problems. A good example is one lie. Unconfessed it can lead to layers of deceit and cover-up, and the liar must constantly worry about being found out.

It's difficult to confess sin. We like to blame others and excuse ourselves. Children need to be taught to take responsibility for their actions. "The devil made me do it" is not acceptable. Help your child to develop a wholesome habit of confessing by modeling it yourself. When you have been impatient or lazy, admit it. Don't just hope your family will overlook it.

Children tend to transfer blame from themselves to inanimate objects, saying things like, "The ball broke the window." Coax the whole story out of your child until he or she can admit, "I did it."

When confronting a child about a misdeed, do not force a confession by asking, "Did you do this?" Chances are the response will be "no." When you catch Rebecca with chocolate icing on her face, state matter-of-factly, "You sampled the cake I made for dessert."

The best way to teach your child the value of confessing is to respond to his or her confession and apology as God does: with forgiveness, sympathy, support and above all with overwhelming love.

CONTRITION: EXPRESSING SORROW

The central and essential piece of reconciliation is contrition. This is a heartfelt sorrow for sin coupled with disgust for the sin committed.

A popular movie some time ago contained the line "Love means never having to say I'm sorry." Actually the opposite is true. One who loves is compelled to say "I'm sorry." Words are powerful symbols. Sincere apologies can mend weak or broken relationships.

Teach your child to say "I'm sorry" to family members and playmates. Let your child hear these words from you after you have hurt him or her or another person. Example is the best teacher.

PURPOSE OF AMENDMENT

Apologies are empty words unless we intend to avoid repeating our faults or sins. If we are really sorry for something, we desire to avoid doing it again. Saying I'm sorry for being an unfaithful spouse, for example, while anticipating the next rendezvous with a lover, is contradictory. True contrition demands a change in behavior and attitude.

When your child has done wrong, lead him or her to promise to try not to do it again. A discussion of the consequences, including the punishment, may help. Work with your child to form a plan of action for the future.

For example, suppose your child is at a party and refuses to share a toy with another child. You might mention the unhappiness of the other child. You can discuss your sadness at being the parent of such a selfish child, the spoiling of the party, the disappointment of Jesus who asks children to love one another. Point out that no one will want to be your child's friend if he or she acts like that. Lead your child to decide to be generous from now on.

MAKING UP

Words are often not sufficient to fully reconcile. Our contrition is borne out in our efforts to do something to counteract the damage we've done and to prevent it from recurring. A man who comes home drunk may have flowers sent to his wife. In society, lawbreakers are sometimes sentenced to do community service. A neighbor whose dog ruins a woman's flower bed might give her a gift certificate to a nursery. This makes up for the sin to a certain extent. It is not punishment. It is a gesture of good will that says, "I wish I could undo what I did."

Your child can form the habit of making up. For young children hugs and kisses are the simplest way to make up. Repentant children can also be led to give small gifts or provide little services as means to repair the harm they've done. You can prompt ideas merely by asking questions like "What do you think you can do to make up to Sarah?" or "How can you let Bob know you're sorry and make him feel better?"

THE SACRAMENT OF HEALING

In general, here's how these same elements come into play in the celebration of the sacrament of reconciliation. We first become aware of our sins by praying to the Holy Spirit and examining our conscience. Major sins surface rather quickly. Pondering the pain sins have caused Jesus and other people gives rise to contrition. Our sins are not forgiven unless we are sorry. We approach the priest in the sacrament and confess our sins, explaining in a conversational way why we think we have committed them. The priest suggests a penance—a prayer or deed—to make up. We pray an act of contrition aloud. After that, the priest raises his hand and says the words of absolution over us. Then, like the ten lepers, the paralytic, the blind, the deaf, and the sinners whom Jesus healed in Israel, we walk away with renewed life and vigor.

It is in discovering the greatness of God's love that our heart is shaken by the horror and weight of sin and begins to fear offending God by sin and being separated from him.

Catechism of the Catholic Church, No. 1432

WHAT TO CONFESS

One day as Father Ed was hearing confessions, a young lad walked into the room. The boy began, "Father, my last confession was a week ago. Since then I haven't committed any sins. I'll try harder this week."

As preparation for celebrating the sacrament of penance, your child is learning what constitutes sins for confession. Sin is any human action or omission that is contrary to God's laws.

When someone asked Jesus what to do to inherit eternal life, Jesus answered, "Keep the commandments." These laws are a gift from God that guide us to wholesome, holy living. They are found in the book of Exodus. God saved the people of Israel and also made a covenant, a solemn agreement with them. On Mount Sinai God gave their leader Moses tablets inscribed with the commandments. In essence God said, "Keep these commandments, and you will be my people and I will be your God."

When asked which was the most important commandment, Jesus explained, "These two: Love God with your whole heart and soul and mind and all your strength, and love your neighbor as yourself." We love God when we keep the first three commandments. We love our neighbor by keeping the last seven.

THE TEN COMMANDMENTS
1. I, the Lord, am your God. You shall not have other gods besides me.
2. You shall not take the name of the Lord, your God, in vain.
3. Keep holy the Sabbath day.

4. Honor your father and your mother.
5. You shall not kill.
6. You shall not commit adultery.
7. You shall not steal.
8. You shall not bear false witness against your neighbor.
9. You shall not covet your neighbor's wife.
10. You shall not covet anything that belongs to your neighbor.

Your child may or may not be asked to memorize the Ten Commandments in class. More important than memorizing the words is understanding their meaning. The teacher will present the core meaning of each law geared to the developmental level of the children. The following keywords may be used:

1. Pray
2. God's Name
3. God's Day
4. Obey
5. Kind
6. and 9. Pure
7. and 10. Honest
8. Truthful

The children should know that if they have stolen anything, they must make restitution. This means replacing what was taken or—if that is not possible—donating an equivalent amount of money to a church or charity.

Strictly speaking, only mortal sins need to be confessed and forgiven in the sacrament of reconciliation. For a sin to be mortal, three conditions must hold: it must be a serious matter, the person must realize its importance, and the person must reflect on its consequences before committing the sin and then decide to do it anyway. It is unlikely that children would commit mortal sin. They should be encouraged, though, to celebrate the sacrament regularly as a means to eliminate sin from their lives and grow in love. The grace of the sacrament will help them resist temptation and live by gospel values.

SINS VERSUS ACCIDENTS

Children tend to think of sin as anything bad that they do or any mistake they make, whether or not it is done on purpose. Your child may need help distinguishing between a deliberate action and an accident. Give examples: breaking a glass because it slipped out of your hands is an accident, while breaking a glass to show you are angry at your mom may be a sin.

SINS VERSUS TEMPTATIONS

You might want to clarify for your child that temptations are not sins. All of us have temptations, urges to do bad things. Even Jesus was tempted. As long as we don't follow this urge and carry out the immoral action, we are innocent. For example, a child may want to talk back to his father but he doesn't. The child does not commit a sin.

The church possesses both water and tears:
the water of baptism, the tears of penance.

Saint Ambrose

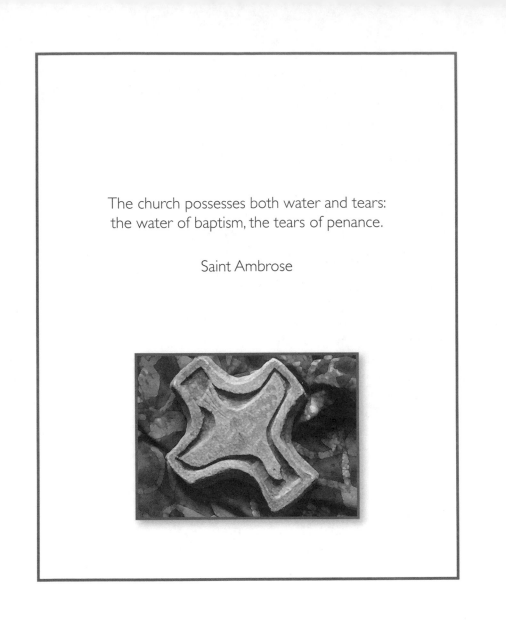

EXAMINATION OF CONSCIENCE

"Know yourself!" is an ancient, wise adage. A preliminary step for the sacrament of reconciliation helps us do this. As immediate preparation for this sacrament, we make an examination of conscience. That is, we review our lives to discover the sins we need to confess and try to root them out. We ponder the areas where we want to be better, more Christ-like persons.

It helps to begin this examination with a prayer to the Holy Spirit for enlightenment. To this person of the Trinity we attribute the work of sanctification—making creation holy. (We say that the Father is in charge of creation and the Son does the work of redemption.) Here is a simple prayer you might teach your child:

Holy Spirit, be with me. Help me to know my sins, be sorry for them, confess them honestly, and avoid them in the future. Amen.

Reflecting on each commandment and how we have kept it is a good method for examining our conscience. We can also reflect on the Beatitudes and the Sermon on the Mount in the gospels and on various virtues. Your child might reflect on the commandments as follows:

1. Have I prayed in the morning and at night?
2. Did I keep from using God's name without respect?
3. Did I celebrate Sunday Eucharist?
4. Did I obey my parents, teachers and others over me? Did I follow laws?

5. Was I kind to others? Did I harm anyone by my words or actions?
6. Did I always tell the truth?
7. Did I keep my promises, unless it would have been wrong to do so?
8. Did I show respect for my body and others' bodies?
9. Did I take or damage anything that didn't belong to me?
10. Did I resent it when others had things I didn't have?

There are books that offer other ways to examine your conscience, usually in the form of questions. No doubt your child's teacher will provide guides for the examination of conscience.

OTHER METHODS

Here are five ways that your child may use to look into his or her heart:

Places: In what ways have I not been God's loving child at home? In school? On the playground? In church?

People: How have I hurt myself? My family members? My friends? Other people? How have I disappointed God?

Time: How have I failed to love in the morning? The afternoon? The evening?

Roles: How have I failed to love as a son or daughter? A family member? A student? A friend?

What would Jesus do (WWJD)? In what ways haven't I acted like Jesus?

One catechist led her children through an examination of conscience using stuffed animals. She held a giraffe and said, "The giraffe has a long neck. Have you ever gone into your brother's or sister's room when you weren't supposed to?" She held a bear and said, "Bears can be mean. Did you growl at your mother, father, brother or sister when you were in a bad mood?" She held an elephant and asked, "Elephants are large and powerful. Were you bossy or did you insist on having your own way?" Other animals can be used in the same way.

DAILY EXAMINATION

A good preparation for confession is to cultivate the habit of making a brief examination of conscience at the end of each day. You might help your child do this by asking at night prayer, "Think if there is any way that you weren't a loving child of God today. Did you do anything that didn't please Jesus?" Then suggest that your child tell Jesus "I'm sorry" and ask his help to be better.

A good conscience is the palace of Christ;
the temple of the Holy Spirit;
the paradise of delight;
the standing Sabbath of the saints.

Saint Augustine of Hippo

THE THREE RITES OF PENANCE

Once a little girl refused to eat her rhubarb at dinner despite all her mom's coaxing. As a final resort, her desperate mom threatened, "If you don't eat it, God will be angry at you." That did not work either. The mother sent the girl to her room. Shortly, a storm came up. As the thunder crashed and the lightning flashed, the mother went to check on her daughter. She expected to find her cowering under the covers. When the mother opened the door, she saw the little girl standing at the window arms akimbo. The girl exclaimed over the noise of the storm, "All this fuss over a little rhubarb!"

Gone are the days when we approach confession fearful of the wrath of God or the wrath of the priest. Someone once said, "The penalty of sin is to face, not the anger of Jesus, but the heartbreak in his eyes." The new Rite of Penance issued in 1973 reflects our new, healthier attitudes toward God and this sacrament.

It's likely that your child will celebrate the sacrament with classmates, using Rite Two. Make sure that he or she knows how to celebrate individually with Rite One as well.

RITE ONE: FOR INDIVIDUAL PENITENTS

Catholics usually celebrate the sacrament of reconciliation individually. The format for this form is as follows:

Welcome

The priest greets your child, and both make the Sign of the Cross. The priest invites your child to trust in God.

God's Word

The priest or your child may read from the Bible about God's forgiving love.

Confession and Penance

1. Your child tells his or her sins. Instead of what was called a "laundry list," this is now more of a conversation. The penitent tries to explain why the sin was committed, and the priest comments or asks questions.
2. The priest exhorts your child to be better and gives some practical advice. Your child can ask any questions.
3. The priest assigns a penance, perhaps after asking your child what he or she thinks should be an appropriate one. Penances are usually prayers, but they can also be actions such as doing an act of kindness for a family member.

Prayer of Contrition and Absolution

1. Your child prays an act of contrition. This may be a standardized prayer or one in your child's own words. Your parish may recommend a particular version. (See pages 55-56 for different versions.)
2. The priest extends his hand and gives absolution. (In face-to-face confession, the priest may lay his hands on your child's head.) Your child makes the Sign of the Cross and responds "Amen."

These are the words of absolution:

God, the Father of mercies, through the death and the resurrection of his Son, has reconciled the world to himself and sent the Holy Spirit among us for the forgiveness of sins; through the ministry of the church may God give you pardon and peace, and I absolve you from your sins in the name of the Father, and of the Son, and of the Holy Spirit.

Praise of God and Dismissal

1. The priest says, "Give thanks to the Lord, for he is good." Your child adds, "His mercy endures forever."
2. The priest may say, "The Lord has freed you from your sins. Go in peace."
3. Your child should say "Thank you."

RITE TWO: FOR SEVERAL PENITENTS WITH INDIVIDUAL CONFESSION AND ABSOLUTION

This rite underlines the communal aspects of sin and reconciliation as penitents celebrate and pray together. Often it is used at parishes during the seasons of Advent and Lent. Here is the format:

1. A greeting and an opening prayer
2. A scripture reading followed by a homily and an examination of conscience
3. General admission of sinfulness and praying of the Lord's Prayer
4. Penitents' going to individual priests for confession, a penance and absolution

5. Praise and thanks to God for mercy
6. Blessing and dismissal

RITE THREE: FOR SEVERAL PENITENTS
WITH GENERAL CONFESSION AND ABSOLUTION

This rite is only for exceptional circumstances, such as when there is a disaster and a priest cannot hear everyone's confession. It is used only with a bishop's permission (although the priest may inform the bishop after the event if the situation was not foreseen). It is like the previous rite, but there is no individual confession, and a common penance and general absolution are given. People who are forgiven mortal sins in this rite are still obliged to confess them to a priest in an individual confession.

The Space

For non-Catholics an intriguing feature of the Catholic faith has been the dark confessional boxes sinners entered to be relieved of their sins. In many churches these boxes have been replaced with reconciliation rooms. Your child will probably enter a lighted room and have two choices for confessing. He or she may kneel behind a screen or sit in a chair facing the priest. The latter arrangement allows for a warmer, more human encounter.

The Confessor

Priests are adept at dealing with very young sinners, especially for first confessions. They try to allay the children's fears and speak gently and encouragingly, reminding the child of God's great love and assuring them that they are forgiven. Your child will feel more comfortable if he or she knows the priest hearing confessions. Explain that the priest is your child's friend.

HOW CAN I PREPARE MY CHILD?

One second-grade boy entered the reconciliation room in fear and trepidation. Immediately sensing that the child was very nervous, the priest tried to put him at ease. As warmly as possible, he welcomed the boy and gently began the sacrament. Suddenly the boy screamed, "I don't want to be in here!" and burst into tears. His mother appeared and rescued the boy (and the priest).

You've actually been preparing your child for this sacrament in numerous ways since birth. Every time you've shown your child unconditional love, you have paved the way for an understanding of God's love. When you taught your child that it's wrong to lie and good to share, you've been forming his or her conscience. When you scolded your child for slapping a sibling or damaging property, you've prepared him or her for confession. If you've taught your child to say "I'm sorry," if you've had your child make up to someone, you've already accomplished a great deal.

MORE WAYS TO PREPARE

Your child's teachers will do their best to present the sacrament as a beautiful, life-giving event. You can reinforce their efforts at home by going over the pages in the religion textbook and discussing them with your child.

Talk about good experiences you've had with the sacrament.

It helps if your child knows the parish priest informally. You might stay after Mass sometime to chat a bit with him or invite him to dinner or a family activity.

If your child's class does not visit the confessional and reconciliation room, take your child on a tour of these yourself. Let your child kneel on the kneeler and sit on the chair.

Your child will be more at ease for first confession if you role-play the rite several times. Respect his or her privacy by using imaginary sins.

Help your child memorize an act of contrition.

Let your child create his or her own act of contrition.

Read your child books or show videos or DVDs that have the themes of reconciliation: unconditional love, forgiveness, contrition. Talk about them.

Four excellent books about love are *The Runaway Bunny* by Margaret Wise Brown, *Love You Forever* by Sheila McGraw, *Nana, Do You Love Me?* by Barbara M. Joosse, and *Guess How Much I Love You* by Sam McBratney.

After you've viewed some television programs, discuss how the characters have kept or not kept God's laws of love. This will help form your child's conscience.

Attend any parent meetings your parish holds regarding the sacrament of penance. You will get ideas and support not only from the presenters but from other parents.

Encourage your child to spend time after receiving the sacrament thanking God for forgiveness. This is also the best time for him or her to do the penance if it is a prayer.

Above all, model God's forgiving love to your child. Be quick to forgive, and avoid bringing up your child's wrongdoing later. Let bygones be bygones.

Sometimes let your child hear you apologize to others and to him or her.

Finally, make it a habit to say "I love you" to your child, perhaps every night at bedtime.

READINESS

Parents are the ones who decide whether or not their child is ready for the sacrament of reconciliation. In 1910, Pope Pius X lowered the age for receiving the sacrament of penance to seven. Nonetheless children develop at different rates. Your child is ready if he or she has a relationship with God, recognizes sin and his or her responsibility for it, and knows that God forgives sin in the sacrament. Incidentally, no child should be forced to celebrate the sacrament.

Nothing in this lost world bears
the impress of the Son of God
so surely as forgiveness.

Alice Carey

QUESTIONS AND ANSWERS

The day of first reconciliation should be a happy day for you and for your child. The following questions and answers are intended to allay some concerns or fears, add to your understanding, and make the day memorable.

QUESTIONS PARENTS MAY HAVE

Are there other ways that sins are forgiven?

Yes, as soon as we are sorry for sin and pray an act of contrition, we are forgiven. The Eucharist contains a ritual of forgiveness. At the beginning of Mass we reflect on our sins, ask for mercy, and pray an act of contrition. Later, before Communion, we pray, "Lord, have mercy." Doing acts of charity is also a means of having sins forgiven. The sacrament of reconciliation, however, is the main method for obtaining forgiveness of sins.

How often should we celebrate the sacrament of reconciliation?

In the past we Catholics went to confession once a week or once a month. Today most of us go less frequently. We are obliged, however, to celebrate the sacrament of reconciliation whenever we have committed mortal sin. In general people like to have their sins forgiven during the church seasons of Advent and Lent and before celebrations such as birthdays and weddings. Going about four times a year is a good policy. You probably want to see that your child celebrates this sacrament rather frequently at first so that it becomes a habit and he or she doesn't forget the ritual.

Must we go to confession each time before we go to Communion?
Although this used to be the practice, it no longer is. No one who is in the state of mortal sin, however, may receive Communion. He or she must first be reconciled to God and the church.

What if my child is afraid and refuses to go to confession?
Have the priest talk with the child to calm his or her fears. He might be able to come up with an acceptable solution for the child.

When can my child celebrate this sacrament again?
Church bulletins list times when priests are available for confessions. They also alert parishioners to communal penance services. In addition anyone may call and set up an appointment with a priest for the celebration of the sacrament.

QUESTIONS YOUR CHILD MAY HAVE

What if I can't hear the priest or don't understand him?
Just ask him to speak louder or to repeat himself. He won't mind.

What if I forget to tell a sin?
You don't have to go back to confess it immediately. If you are sorry for this sin, God will forgive you in other ways, like through the Eucharist. You can confess it the next time you celebrate the sacrament of reconciliation if you wish. Even if your mind goes blank and you can't think of anything to confess, God and the priest understand.

What if I forget what my penance is?

You might give yourself a penance and then tell the priest next time what you did. It's important to do your penance as soon as possible so you don't forget it.

Will the priest ever tell anyone what I say?

No, priests are bound by what is called the seal of the sacrament. This means they must never reveal what people have told them in confession.

What if I can hear someone else's confession?

Try to distance yourself far enough so you can't hear. If you can't help hearing, you are bound not to tell what you heard.

Will the priest be upset by my sins or angry with me?

No, he has probably heard everything already. He sins, too, and understands how we are weak and tempted.

Would a priest ever not forgive my sins?

The priest denies absolution only if he knows that the person confessing the sin is not really sorry. He would know this by talking to the person about the sin and learning that the person intends to keep committing it.

Does the priest scold you?

The priest is happy that you are sorry for your sins. In confession he tries to help you be a better person and love God more.

It is true that we cannot be free from sin,
but at least let our sins not be always the same.

Saint Teresa of Avila

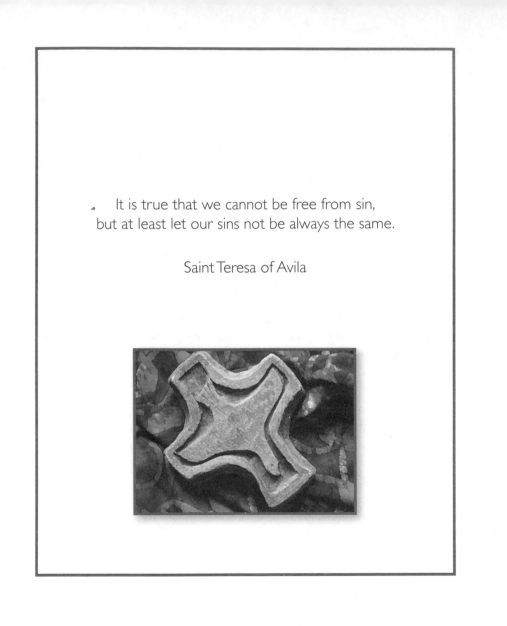

HOW CAN WE
CELEBRATE THE EVENT?

Your child will understand the significance of the sacrament of reconciliation by the significance you give it in your life and home. Here are three ideas for highlighting the event of first reconciliation.

1. **Go to confession yourself when your child does.** Your parish program may allow families to celebrate the sacrament on the same day as the children. If not, arrange to celebrate the sacrament on a day near your child's celebration. Make sure that your child knows you are doing this and why. Your witness will speak volumes.

   Perhaps you have not gone to confession for a long time because of busyness, laziness, reluctance to change, embarrassment or a bad experience. This is the ideal time for you to put your life in order and return to God, who waits for you with love and concern.

   If you are not Catholic or for some reason are unable to confess your sins and be forgiven when your child does, you still may go to the priest for a few words and a blessing.

2. **Hold a family reconciliation.** Some families have the practice of asking pardon of one another before celebrating the sacrament of reconciliation. On the day of your child's first con-

fession or the evening before, gather as a family. Simply take turns stating how you have not been a loving family member and apologizing to those you have hurt. Then conclude by saying the Our Father together. You might do this in the context of a longer ritual. See pages 55-56.

3. **Celebrate the event.** After the sacrament of reconciliation, go out for ice cream or pizza or to a restaurant. You might also throw a little party that includes your child's favorite foods. Invite your child's godparents.

   Decorate your dining room or living room with a dove, a symbol of the Holy Spirit and of peace. (You can also display this dove each time you celebrate the sacrament in the future.) You may prefer to make and display a banner or poster about forgiveness.

   As a memento of the day, give your child an item related to a Bible forgiveness story: a toy sheep for the lost sheep, a coin for the lost coin, or a ring for the story of the prodigal son. A congratulations card is also in order.

SCRIPTURE READINGS
FOR RECONCILIATION

You have prepared for your child's first celebration of the sacrament of reconciliation by reading this book. Another way you can prepare is to read and ponder the following scripture passages related to this sacrament. Arrange some private time to read a passage and the comments that follow it. Then consider what the passage means to you and your life. Let your thoughts give rise to resolutions that will help you be a better Christian parent for your child. You may record your resolutions on page 59. Every now and then read your resolutions and review how you are keeping them.

Have mercy on me, God in your goodness;
in your abundant compassion blot out my offense.
Wash away all my guilt;
from my sin cleanse me.

Cleanse me with hyssop, that I may be pure;
wash me, make me whiter than snow.

Turn away your face from my sins; blot out all my guilt.
A clean heart create for me, God;
renew in me a steadfast spirit.
Do not drive me from your presence,
nor take from me your holy spirit.

Psalm 51: 3-4, 9, 11-13

David, the great king of Israel and ancestor of Jesus, was also a great sinner. He had an affair with the wife of one of his soldiers. When she became pregnant by David, he arranged to have her husband killed in battle. A sorrowful David composed Psalm 51, a classic prayer of contrition, expressing David's repentance.

This psalm demonstrates well what is in our hearts when we are sorry for sin. In the psalm we appeal to God's goodness and compassion for mercy. The word *compassion* is from the Latin for "to suffer with." God, in a manner of speaking, feels our pain. We rely on God's love for us to wash away our sins, to blot them out quickly and completely. We desire a renewed innocence. We ask God to make us as white as snow, to give us a clean heart and a steadfast spirit.

Deep down we long to be with God. This alone brings real and lasting joy. Knowing that sin separates us from God, we pray for forgiveness and the grace to resolve to go forward, faithful to our calling to be God's holy people.

JESUS HEALS SINNERS

And there people brought to him a paralytic lying on a stretcher. When Jesus saw their faith, he said to the paralytic, "Courage, child, your sins are forgiven." At that, some of the scribes said to themselves, "This man is blaspheming." Jesus knew what they were thinking, and said, "Why do you harbor evil thoughts? Which is easier, to say, 'Your sins are forgiven,' or to say, 'Rise and walk'? But that you may know that the Son of Man has authority on earth to forgive sins"—he then said to the paralytic, "Rise, pick up your stretcher, and go home." He rose and went home.
Matthew 9:2-7

Jesus is our source of life and wellness. The paralyzed man was helpless, not only physically but spiritually. Mired in sin, he could not function as a healthy human being. Concerned friends brought him to the Divine Physician, the same way you are taking your child to Jesus in this sacrament of healing.

Jesus' words uplift and heal the man. He tells the paralytic to have courage and addresses him familiarly as "child." Reading the man's heart, Jesus immediately forgives his sins. Aware that only God can forgive sins, bystanders accuse Jesus of blasphemy. In reply, Jesus proves he has the right and authority to forgive sins. He works a miracle which reveals his divinity. He heals the paralytic.

In a way Jesus says to us, "Rise and walk," in the sacrament of reconciliation. Sin paralyzes us, shrinks our self-esteem, makes us want to curl up in a corner. At Jesus' forgiving words, we can stand tall with dignity once more. We can walk on.

JESUS SEEKS OUT THE LOST

He came to Jericho and intended to pass through the town. Now a man there named Zacchaeus, who was a chief tax collector and also a wealthy man, was seeking to see who Jesus was; but he could not see him because of the crowd, for he was short in stature. So he ran ahead and climbed a sycamore tree in order to see Jesus, who was about to pass that way. When he reached the place, Jesus looked up and said to him, "Zacchaeus, come down quickly, for today I must stay at your house." And he came down quickly and received him with joy. When they all saw this, they began to grumble, saying, "He has gone to stay at the house of a sinner." But Zacchaeus stood there and said to the Lord, "Behold, half of my possessions, Lord, I shall give to the poor, and if I have extorted anything from anyone I shall repay it four times over." And Jesus said to him, "Today salvation has come to this house because this man too is a descendant of Abraham. For the Son of Man has come to seek and to save what was lost."
Luke 19:1-10

Jesus changed plans. Instead of passing through Jericho, he decided to stay at the house of Zacchaeus, a sinner. Again Jesus goes out of his way and against public opinion to save someone. He sees potential for good in this man who swindles his own people. Jesus seeks out Zacchaeus hidden in the sycamore branches and favors him with his presence. Jesus tells Zacchaeus to come down quickly; he wants the man to be saved as soon as possible. Zacchaeus's response is twofold: he accepts the invitation with joy and declares how he will change. He will make up for his past sins four times more than required.

This is Jesus' mission: to bring salvation to every person who is up a tree. It's up to us to choose to respond, to make ourselves worthy of welcoming Jesus into the home of our hearts.

Through grace the short Zacchaeus becomes a big man in the eyes of Jesus and the townspeople. Encountering Jesus prompts him to give half of his wealth to the poor. What change in your lifestyle is called for as you live as a friend and follower of Jesus?

JESUS SAVES A CONDEMNED WOMAN

> *Then the scribes and the Pharisees brought a woman who had been caught in adultery and made her stand in the middle. They said to him, "Teacher, this woman was caught in the very act of committing adultery. Now in the law, Moses commanded us to stone such women. So what do you say?" They said this to test him, so that they could have some charge to bring against him. Jesus bent down and began to write on the ground with his finger. But when they continued asking him, he straightened up and said to them, "Let the one among you who is without sin be the first to throw a stone at her." Again he bent down and wrote on the ground. And in response, they went away one by one, beginning with the elders. So he was left alone with the woman before him. Then*

Jesus straightened up and said to her, "Woman, where are
they? Has no one condemned you?" She replied, "No one, sir."
Then Jesus said, "Neither do I condemn you. Go, [and] from
now on do not sin any more."

John 8:3-11

According to the Jewish law, the woman brought before Jesus should have been punished. Imagine the lecture Jesus could have given her. Because Jesus has incredible mercy, however, the adulteress is free to leave with only an admonishment to sin no more. Instead of death she receives life.

The men who accused the woman were also sinners. It's been proposed that Jesus wrote reminders of their sins in the sand, and that is why they slipped away. Jesus and his mother Mary (by privilege of the Immaculate Conception) are the only persons not tainted by sin. Although Jesus qualified to cast a stone, he chose not to condemn the woman but to offer her another chance.

We can expect the same merciful treatment when we approach Jesus in the sacrament of reconciliation. If we come with humble contrition and sorrow, he does not condemn us but encourages us to start anew. As Christians who model their lives on Jesus, it follows that we extend to sinners the same mercy he shows.

PRAYERS FOR RECONCILIATION

ACT OF CONTRITION FROM THE RITE OF PENANCE
My God,
I am sorry for my sins with all my heart.
In choosing to do wrong
and failing to do good,
I have sinned against you,
whom I should love above all things.
I firmly intend, with your help,
to do penance,
to sin no more,
and to avoid whatever leads me to sin. Amen.

SHORT ACT OF CONTRITION
O my God, I am very sorry for all my sins, because they displease you, who are all-good and deserving of all my love. With your help, I will sin no more. Amen.

ACT OF CONTRITION FROM THE MASS
I confess to almighty God and to you, my brothers and sisters, that I have sinned through my own fault. In my thoughts and in my words, in what I have done, and in what I have failed to do; and I ask blessed Mary, ever virgin, all the angels and saints, and you, my brothers and sisters, to pray for me to the Lord our God.

TRADITIONAL ACT OF CONTRITION

O my God, I am heartily sorry for having offended you. And I detest all my sins because of your just punishment. But most of all because they offend you, O God, who are all-good and deserving of all my love. I firmly resolve with the help of your grace to sin no more and to avoid the near occasions of sin. Amen.

A FAMILY CELEBRATION OF RECONCILIATION

- Gather in a circle. Play soft music and light a candle if you wish.

- Read 1 John 3:18-24 or 1 John 1:5-22 or a scripture story about God's mercy. (See pages 15-16, 49-54, 58.)

- Leader: "Jesus wants us to love one another. Sometimes we have not been loving family members. We have hurt one another. This has damaged the peace and joy of our family life. Let us now ask forgiveness."

- Members admit ways they have not been loving and apologize to one another.

- Pray the Our Father holding hands or with arms around one another.

- Exchange a sign of peace: a handshake, hugs or a group hug.

- Parents bless the children by tracing the Sign of the Cross on their foreheads. (Children may bless the parents too.)

- Sing a song such as "Peace Is Flowing like a River."

Additional Ideas

1. After the scripture is read, members write on a large paper heart how they contribute to the wellbeing of the family. After the leader's introductory words, the heart is torn into several large pieces. At the end of the ritual the heart is taped back together and displayed.

2. Members write what they are sorry for on slips of paper. These are crumpled up, put into a metal container, and burned.

3. On paper hearts members write how they intend to improve. They keep the hearts on their dressers or nightstands as a reminder.

4. State the admission of sin in the form of a litany. The leader names a general offense and everyone responds, "Forgive our selfishness." Example:

For the times we keep others waiting...
For not doing our chores...
For being grouchy...
For not showing appreciation...
For hurting others' feelings...
For insisting on having my way...
For being too sensitive...
For taking the heat for myself...

5. Here are some more scripture stories about God's forgiveness:

- Matthew 9:9-13
- Luke 15:1-7
- Luke 15:8-10
- Luke 15:11-32
- Ezekiel 34:11-16

RESOLUTIONS FOR PARENTS

To help my child celebrate the sacrament of reconciliation
now and in the future, I resolve the following:

RECORD OF RECONCILIATION

_____ _____celebrated
(Name)

the Sacrament of Reconciliation

on _____ at_____ _____
(Date)   (Church)

with _____
(Priest)

Significant features (others present, how we marked the occasion):

_____

_____

_____

_____

_____

_____

_____

_____

Note: For more in-depth information about the Sacrament of Reconciliation, you might consult the *Catechism of the Catholic Church*. Chapter Two of Part Two, "The Celebration of the Christian Mystery," is about this sacrament.

OTHER BOOKS IN THIS SERIES

THE GIFT OF BAPTISM

TOM SHERIDAN

A welcoming book that teaches parents about the meaning of the sacrament and helps them understand their role as parents. 64 pages, paperback, $5.95

THE GIFT OF CONFIRMATION

SISTER KATHLEEN GLAVICH

Explanation and suggestions for parents of children being confirmed, including much of the information contained in *The Gift of Confirmation Sponsors*. 80 pages, paperback, $4.95

THE GIFT OF THE ANOINTING OF THE SICK

SISTER KATHLEEN GLAVICH

Discusses the power behind this sacrament and explains how it is administered today. For people preparing for the anointing of the sick as well as their family members and friends. 64 pages, paperback, $4.95

THE GIFT OF GODPARENTS

TOM SHERIDAN

Information about the sacrament of baptism and the responsibilities of godparenting are blended with touching stories and suggestions. 96 pages, paperback, $5.95

THE GIFT OF CONFIRMATION SPONSORS

SISTER KATHLEEN GLAVICH

Explanation and suggestions for those chosen to be sponsors for children being confirmed, including much of the information contained in *The Gift of Confirmation*, but aimed specifically at sponsors. 80 pages, paperback, $4.95

THE GIFT OF HOLY COMMUNION

SISTER KATHLEEN GLAVICH

A book that explains the Eucharist to parents of children receiving Communion for the first time and gives them the words to use when talking with their children about the sacrament. 80 pages, paperback, $4.95

AVAILABLE FROM BOOKSELLERS OR CALL 800-397-2282